FABER NEW

Toby Martinez de las Rivas

———

faber and faber

First published in 2009
by Faber and Faber Ltd
Bloomsbury House
74–77 Great Russell Street
London WC1B 3DA

Typeset by Faber & Faber Ltd
Printed in England by T. J. International Ltd, Padstow, Cornwall

ACKNOWLEDGEMENTS

The author would like to thank New Writing North for
the Andrew Waterhouse Award, *Ambit*, *Dreamcatcher*
and *The Wolf*, where some of the poems have appeared,
and Gillian Allnutt, Melanie Challenger and Joolz Denby
for their work on the poems.

A CIP record for this book
is available from the British Library

ISBN 978-0-571-24996-1

2 4 6 8 10 9 7 5 3 1

Contents

Song

An 'arrogant little tool', that was Migdale.

All five foot four of him.

Always scratching his head and looking pained and
    adjusting himself.

The last time I saw him, it was his well-fed silhouette
straddling the gate in half-light,

'too busy' to come in good time for the birth, and 'too poor'
    for the vet,
instead he came like a thief in the night,

shooing the crows and draping an inverse, eyeless thing
over his shoulder with disdain like a soiled boa.

As he sloped away, his back grew dark with burst caul,
    the slipped halo
of that 'poor fellow'.

Goodbye, little song.

Goodbye, Migdale.

They said in the village you were an absentee landlord,
    a shirker, a fool.

But nightfall and sun-up wait at your beck and call.

Blackdown Song

In front of the gate whose tubes hummed in the wind
like owls hooing each other across a dark field, Isabel,
was the firepit's tract of soot-soft & snow-white ashes.

It went deeper than you knew, after years of bonfires,
dusks when sightly wings of paper flared in a woosh
of sparks & ghosted into darknesse like minor stars.

Beyond the singing gate lay the dark field which ate
the bodies of lambs & threw up the bleached fans
of pigeon wings: the grass grew red in those places.

I dug the pit with a shovel & scooped bucketloads
to feed my father's garden which drew down silver
mouthfuls of ash & the tangled brown potato haulms.

All the while the gate hummed tunelessly in the wind;
tunelessly, but with range: high & low, long & short,
disconnected, artless, dumb life struggling into song.

I struck so reckless, Isabel – hot, one-handed, peeved,
& clanged a rock that hung in earth as consciousness is
said to inhere in the self, or the self to hang in the body.

High, low, long, short: my arms went dead, a dazed bird
burst from my skull, the rock, humped, deaf to the blow.
A brilliant ringing in the blade secured itself to that axis.

Poem, Three Weeks After Conception

The sky will be shaped like a bow when you crane your neck to
    pray into it.
Roofless, but not burned. Though black, spangled.

Your hair will be the white spray at High Force,
teeth pebbles in the vent.

You will escape the ogre of psoriasis that lives on the knees,
elbowcaps, genitals and face.

For you the stars have already locked into place.

For you the blue coltsfoot in the allotment will be an electrical wonder.

The red kite, wolf and bear will return to the borders in numbers.

You will be buried in a country far away, a country like home,
of absolute rainfall.

Beneath a late moon, unfurling.

You shall witness the domination of Jerusalem.

The capsize of London.

I pray that I will never hit or humiliate you,
for whom the best wine in the world will be pressed in Kent.

Who will live to see supermarkets dictating military policy to
    governments.

Our Lady of Gateshead, watch over us.

Self-Portrait on The Levels

A field of water the sun stares up
from with cold, undiminished ferocity.
Unconscious of its own image
in the wind breaking, breaking and re-
forming, how barely it seems to live
the automatic and suicidal gift
of its self-burning, the blind necessity
of love, broken and re-forming.
The elegant feathers of grass bow to it
coyly, above a flight of ducks in-
carnadine as nipple-heads, their under-
sides beating to the rush of shot.
Uncoppiced, a line of Black Mauls
wanders to the horizon, trailing fingers
through the surface of a rare heaven –
as if patiently for the season when
they shall be hurdles, and withy men.

The First Appearance of the Angel of Death, in His Aerial Form

Terror, I remember where I saw you first: on a cliff-edge
Above Milford Haven, all the grass yellow with buttercups
Bar at the black entrance to an antique ferro-concrete pillbox
Where endless traipsings corrupted the earth into a wet splurge.

You reared up above the cliff, your belly sleek and grey,
I fell into that square black slot and fainted clean away.
With a *ha ha ha* and a *ho ho ho*, my father brought me round,
My eyes were anchored in the dark, my body to the ground.

O, that was the summer of my father's father's passing,
The policeman with a face like the picture of a policeman's face
Waiting in the whiteness of the door and my father repeating
He's gone? He's gone? and so he had, to a silentswaying place.

The summer the swept-winged and beroundled Vulcan roared
And the yellow grass and everything and I fell into darkness.

from Instructions on How to Raise the Dead

brother, the king, knaves, the year the war ended, *p*liancy,   X
return, sophomore, repetition, furrow, the tower, rewards,
infancy, number of the beast, kingdom, failsafe, paraclete,
her scent, sarah, the rose, satan, falling leaves, power, lip,
burned tree, the lamb, a cloud, halo, goshawk, sword arm,
loosestrife, the bear, ploughshare, they will never be able
to say, court of the burning star, hand of peace, sorrow, to
love, bombsight, valleys, queen of hearts, false aspect, the
double image, the serpent, a killing field, the rising moon,
trickery, hautepsalm, salted bacon, lorca, flowers, selfless,
the bee, ragged stone, the mouth is empty, the pin, primate,
white dove, positivism, skirmish, thank heaven, pun, rame,
XVI   the world, the dragon, sparrows, jeoffrey, bar, the burn, air,
watermint, the flesh, death, the witch, a cloud, mercy, roan,
instruments of joie, the seat, fealty, my faraway, fie, enoch,
nineteen, asthenia cold, stop sign, the fool, mother of pearl,
the arrow, a little night music, cowardice, bang, black gold,
cremation, hedge of spears, qi, as the waves break, oratory,
a full ten seconds later, tendernesse, hunting pike, relenting,
VII   the falstaff, wrens, between her legs, the poets, rage, closed
XIV   door, falsehood, fire, the house of life is following *a*fter you

XXII

Twenty-One Prayers for Weak
or Fabulous Things

When animals which lived under water afterwards live in air,
their bodies change almost entirely, so as hardly to be known
by any one mark of resemblance to their former figure; as, for
example, from worms and caterpillars to flies and moths . . .
These changes take place in consequence of the unalterable
rule, that the body be fitted to the state . . . Now our present
bodies are by no means fitted for heaven.
– WILLIAM PALEY, *Sermon XXVII, Of the State after Death*

'I was once acquainted with a tall man,' he said to me at last,
'that had no name either and you are certain to be his son and
the heir to his nullity and all his nothings.'
– FLANN O'BRIEN, *The Third Policeman*

As snow falls, as the first snow of this year falls & falls
        beyond all light & knowledge, I pray for Rufus
corrupted by blood parasites, whose liver is corrupted
        & whose eyes are uncorrupted by swivelling in
the weak light. I speak this prayer into the inflamed sun.

Secondly, I pray for stooping David who sees his dead
        sister walking in the bedroom each morning up
& down, a shadow of herself. I pray for all things that
        shed their skins: for snakes, for cicadas & silk
worms clasped to branches & hidden in rattling bushes.

Thirdly, I pray for a babbling drunk fisherman wearing
        no pants, dredged from the Tyne, who swore
everafter that by praying to Cuddy, he was able to call
        silver trout from the river, to throw themselves
from their element into his: & there they flop, gasping.

Fourthly, I pray for a war protester picketing the Sage,
    whose banner is stitched with cluster bombs
like falling seeds having the real viridian sting of black
    pansies opening. I pray for all things that open
& follow the sun, its star-track raked in the winter sky.

Fifthly, I pray for the ghost of Rene & the living ghost
    of Mary in the final blank stage of Alzheimer's,
nodding, clucking & fumbling. I pray for the sunflower,
    thin petals opening, head bowed, face nodding
imperceptibly nightward. It has arms, too, to hold itself.

Sixthly, I pray for a humble Yellowhammer who when
    he sings, sings in English, 'a little bit of bread
& no cheese.' This is acknowledgement of the body's
    need & the body's need to sing. I pray for the
ghost of Barry MacSweeney, which has a bird's throat.

Seventhly, I pray for the sparrow, tongue-cut, whirring,
    who in Egypt had a jackal's garish blunt head
& carried dead children across the river, but in England
    he's a merry fat fellow. I listen to his declining
brotherhood at Middlezoy: there is one fewer every day.

Eighthly, I pray for Jimmy who strokes Mary's hands &
    looks into Mary's empty shell each Wednesday,
also on her birthday & at Christmas. I pray for all things
    whose meat's scooped out. 8 is a sign of infinity
& also the sum of YHVH, double barrels of emptinesse.

Ninthly, I pray to the memory of the prodigious monster
    of Ravenna & prophesy with Arthur Clarke that
one day people will do away with their bodies & encode
    themselves as quanta or pure mental self-image.
The wing is for fickleness, the claw greed, the horn pride.

Tenthly, I pray for the last few seconds of a cold August,
  when the world is stilled, a sullen body of water
that brings forth flies & creeping beasts to my fingertips,
  my tongue a water-snail with soft horns poking
its head from between my lips, prince of dusk & muscle.

My eleventh prayer is for Migdale checking the hooves
  of his sheep for rot separating the hoof's heel,
sole & wall from their attachments to the foot, & for the
  sheep like amputees hobbling & nibbling at
lung flukes & brain worms: & some fall down, shaking.

My twelfth prayer is for the fledgling rooks shawled by
  ants beneath the nests. For the membra over the
black pods of their eyes. For their crackable elbows and
  white beaks. For the boot I bring down on them.
Let me love best of all the creeping things that creepeth.

My thirteenth prayer is for the memory of Nicholas Flüe
  who saw the face of the lord deformed by anger,
& whose own face was transformed into a deathmask by
  that vision of lacerations. He shuts his house to
light. *Today even the sparrows cannot bear to look at me.*

My fourteenth prayer is for psoriatics: for all the world is
  a clear mirror they fall apart in day after day, for
every beautiful thing grows to a scaly deformity & even
  the face of the sun glows scabrous & repugnant:
but like pythons they slough off their skins & slither out.

My fifteenth prayer is for you, Isabel, eaten by distance.
  I see the shape of your pumping heart & it is the
shape of the winter cherry shaken by a heave of wind; its
  blossom blows off, acquiescence in the bough,
but my heart is a bird high in the canopy: a false lapwing.

My sixteenth prayer is for the solitary writhing bee that I
found in the allotment, like an aeronaut slumped
in the collapsed riggings of his machine: he thumped his
sting once into the sodden ground to vent his fury
& is free to go. I am not free to go, nor will I be released.

My seventeenth prayer is to the memory of Christopher
Smart kneeling in a cloud of honeybees at Stain-
drop to pray, or carving the Song to David into the walls
at Bedlam with a workaday burin – a nail or key –
& with his fingertips rubbing charcoal into the scratches.

My eighteenth prayer is for the glass ghosts of Rudolf &
Leo Blashka, combinations of moonlight & utile
organ, tendrils of pink glass hunting down their prey by
security light and night vision: an inward ocean.
I say this prayer as the clouds shift to smother the moon.

My nineteenth prayer is for that one who sat in watch on
the top stair when the child came home, to guard
against the visit of the devil, whose raw stare counteracts
supernatural malice and who, after the dragon &
the owl, is the most canny & puissant of all living beasts.

My twentieth prayer is cobbled from nineteen fragments:
four of flesh, two of wood, one is a shred of paper
from which a peregrine takes wing: another is its falling.
Ten are made of air & the eighth means nothing.
There is a gap between each one where the breath comes.

Lastly, I pray for the makers of prayers, which are poems
we say to ourselves in the hard times, cold times,
dry times, tucked in tenements & tower blocks, in the lock-
ups of our bodies, between the soil & sky, falling
& falling like snow flakes beyond all light & knowledge.

Free Dialect Poem with Every Collection

Ah dinnieken hoo thes aw began, ah think ah jist
woke up a bonny braw morn tae fin' mah sassenach
accent hud fa'en awa' an' haur ah was spikin' Scots.
Mah guidwife thooght she was in uir scratcher wi'
anither cheil at first, she gae a scream when ah spoke.

'Rabbie,' she said tae me, 'yer the Oxford Professur
ay Poetry, ye cannae gang tae wark soondin' leik
a vagabond who's got naethin' to cowre his sham
but a sporran, Rabbie.' 'Guidwife,' ah said, 'it's
aw th' rage tae write a wee bit in the Scots tongue,

an' ye weel ken ah was born a mile frae Auld Reekie
an' grew up as a committed socialist an' nationalist,
th' only a body tae be foond in aw the Haem Coonties.
An' ah hae ne'er forgotten mah Scottish roots, an' hoo
the wee sassenach tadgers butchered uir Scots leid, hen.'

Sae here's hoo ye dae it, reader, in order ay priority.
First ay aw, ye cultivate th' soft soonds ay th' lowlands
until burds begin tae swoon when ye spick tae them.
Next, ye write yer poems, than write a wee glossary
at th' back explainin' yer tumshies an' twangers an'

tottie scones tae the numpties who dinnae ken th' true
heart an' sool ay us Scots adrift in thes foreign lain.
Then, ye dae an interview an' bevvy some bucky an'
caw th' crack an' after that ye can help me pull oot aw
th' fifty poond noots that are wedged up mah jacksie.

Things I Have Loved

The Flea, principally,
pronounced Flay.

Smart, who disliked clean linen,
whom Johnson would as lief pray with as anyone.

Paper aeroplanes like prayers in childhood, winged, rising, risen.

Headflare in multi-directional light, that Blackdown morning
the lamb was born, dead, beside his sister.

XXVI March,
the jute-sack and the shovel, as if by magic.

My never-to-be-born daughter, of the House of Míro Quesada.

How her body bucked like a beast dragged by its neck from the holt
when I touched it as instructed.

Each breath, a mist or brief rapt element, swept up,
escaped.

Fenlight, shivering in its seat.

Man Praying, King's Cross, 34°

I will rise in this heat and rod myself south,
muscular forearms with their black guard hairs
shoving beneath the elbow-cuffs of my blue shirt
confidently, only cut by the brown leather band
of my watch ticking like a banked departure board.
People drain around me like the tide receding
around a sandbank, or like grains of sand dragged
very beautifully but helplessly into the offing:
a boy with chipped black fingernails and hair
swept from his eyes, smeared black Chloé eyeliner:
a pregnant woman like the *Santissima Trinidad*,
straining serenely windward, all her sails billowing.
In caelo, in caelo I see all these forms surrendering
themselves to my angel posture, clenched fingers
forming four perfect scarp-and-tarns, two thumbs,
the thumb-knuckles pressed up against my lips,
head bowed, knees on the floor of gum and muck
among throstling bodies going down into the floodlit
dark, soaring of fahrenheit, everything burning like
hellfire, beautiful. Bermondsey, Angel, Deptford.
I will rise in this oven's ferocity like bread, leaven.

We are the Borg

Then, our bodies will be metal and light, durable alloys: tungsten,
        zirconium, tantalum. The mind will sing in its prime,
    quantum state. The voicebox will correspond with perfect pitch.
If it does not respond with perfect pitch, it will be replaced.

    Matthew, your arms *will be* as flexible as your mind *is*.
    Your body will roll with the punches, being gone.

    Matthew, there is no humanity, only an institution of selves
    competing blindly in the same direction, against peace.

Matthew, the doctrine of humanism is a false religion,
and so we are in the psychological fire all of our lives.

    Because: how can we still believe in destiny knowing
    ourselves to be the technological creations of bacteria?

    Matthew, despite this, I believe that by accident or greed, one
    day, we will make our bodies function without food or light.

Matthew, I believe that this benefit will be the unintended
result of military applications, gene and nanotech weapons,

airbursts, retreats into shelter plastered with Renaissance posters,
        plates littering the table, overturned cups, rat tails
    whipping the corners, lamplight, sootstreak, crying, revolutions,
coups, atrocities, extinctions, till we are all changed,

till our bodies are substituted and healed, this much I promise you.

The White Road

for Mary Bullen, memoryless

Name the constellations for us,
The tracks they drag through the night
Like a hawk's mind stripping a rat

I

Beneath the holed roof showing stars
    rats run through the attic,
rock back on haunches whispering
    into a spread fan of claws,
or scamper with swift, witless intent
    up the tattered remainders,
the slashed fabrics peed on, despoiled.

On the high days, Father Enright spoke
    about the primal self: how
it was like a rat one had to tame – hands
    in gloves, a string about its
neck – to break it in the house of its flesh.

II

'You are spinning,' I said to her. Her eyes
glanced over me, making no effort of attention.
'Yes,' she said.
– D. H. LAWRENCE, *Twilight in Italy*

Marquesa of the torched estate,
    ascend the trap in sudden poverty,
settle your skirts, smooth them
    on the seat and wait most patiently.

Confusion rules all the desolate.
    The flogged and the footloose ruin
the house, tear hangings down.
    You are left with your Sunday best.

They have nailed your husband
    to the branches of the ragged oak,
and the lamb has changed places
    with the tiger, nothing is as it was.

Time flows beyond reckoning.
    There, there, pat my hands, my head,
your eyes vacated, blank glass
    where, occasionally, a child pauses.

Is it the rat of the body running
    blindly up tunnels, sniffing dead ends,
personality's armature unpicked
    twist by twist, disproving the gospels?

Set the trap in motion, harnessed
    to the world which turns a frightsome
eye to regard you over the meat
    of its shoulder, then turns to plod on.

At the juncture of the crosshatch,
    take the white road where the white
wind blows through white leaves
    and troubles your hair like wild garlic.

Take the white road where love
    is coterminous with flesh, unsupernal,
unlifted above the vesicle of its
    own surge and rush and failing like it.

Wave back without a smile, that's
    right, let the fingers do their own thing,
pluck at the lap aimlessly, remember
    the movements of crocheting or patch.

III

    Don't fret,
Mary Bullen, godcundnes is in the world.
    No cables of lightning fork
across your abyssal, graveyard of names
    and faces whose memory
rides off into an absence the size of a life.

    Mary, you were married in a chapel
near Versailles after the liberation.
    Jimmy drew it with pastels,
his despatch bike meeting its shadow
    on the whitewashed wall,
war-heavy like a warhorse broadsided,
    but attentive to each nudge
as he took off down the dappled lane
    in a roar of dust, what
a dish, past horses blown into trees
    with bits of half-track,
flesh and metal wind-chimes chiming,
    promising he'd be back
and good as his word.

    Godcundnes is in the world:
don't turn away from it. Don't turn away,
    as the kingfisher escapes the river
with its beakful of silver elvers,
    and the wren its thorny custody
in a flash of wings and black underbelly.